Hutchinson Checkbook Series

Punctuation

Philip Payne

Series Editor
Roy Blatchford

Hutchinson
London Sydney Auckland Johannesburg

Other titles in the series

Comprehension Bill Deller and Michael Taylor
Spelling Martin Tucker
Summary Ken Methold and Roy Blatchford
Writing Linda Cookson

Hutchinson & Co (Publishers) Ltd

An imprint of the Hutchinson Publishing Group

62-65 Chandos Place, London WC2N 4NW

Hutchinson Group (Australia) Pty Ltd
89-91 Albion Street, Surry Hills, New South Wales 2010, Australia

Hutchinson Group (NZ) Ltd
32-34 View Road, PO Box 40-086, Glenfield, Auckland 10

Hutchinson Group (SA) (Pty) Ltd
PO Box 337, Bergvlei 2012, South Africa

First published 1983
Reprinted 1985, 1986, 1989

© Philip Payne 1983

Set in 10/12 Century Schoolbook
by Oxprint Ltd, Oxford

Printed and bound in Great Britain by
Scotprint Ltd., Musselburgh

British Library Cataloguing in Publication Data

Payne, Philip
  Punctuation. - (Checkbooks for English)
  1. English Language - Punctuation
  I. Title   II. Series
  421   PE1450

ISBN 0-09-149281-5

Contents

Introduction
1. Sentence and full stop — 5
2. Capital letters — 9
3. Comma — 13
4. Question mark, Exclamation mark — 17
5. Apostrophe 1 – to show possession or relationship — 22
6. Apostrophe 2 – for letters left out — 26
7. Speech marks – inverted commas — 32
8. Brackets (parentheses) — 37
9. Colon — 41
10. Semi-colon — 44
11. Dash — 47
12. Prefixes, Hyphens — 50
13. Business letters — 53
14. Cutting it short – three useful abbreviations — 57
15. Revision — 61

You will find the self-test answers to each chapter at the end of the previous chapter.

Introduction

One or two of the practice sections in this book, particularly those concerned with letter writing, are intended to be written out. As for the rest, the writer believes that oral practice is more interesting, more useful, and corrects errors as they are made rather than encouraging the pupil to fix them firmly in his mind by repetition. Self-test sections are for the student learning or revising by himself. Information and practice sections can be used for group work, with students working together over problems, thus putting the emphasis on co-operative work rather than competition.

The book began as a teaching aid at Burnt Mill School in Harlow when I was head of English there. I am indebted to my successor, Dave Huband, for improving it and helping to prepare it for publication.

Philip Payne

Sentence and full stop

Quick reference

A SENTENCE – BEGINS WITH A CAPITAL LETTER
– ENDS WITH A FULL STOP
– MAKES SENSE

EXAMPLES: She smiled at his joke.

Their singing was noisy.

Love of money is the root of all evil.

Information

Purpose

The full stop tells you that a sentence is complete. It tells you to pause, even though your eyes go straight on to the words following.

Start each sentence with a capital letter and put a full stop (or question mark or exclamation mark) at the end. This helps people to understand what you have written.

How to recognize a sentence

A sentence is a group of words that makes sense by itself.

Here are five:

The wind is cold tonight.
We ought to light the fire.
Do you know where the matches are?
I'll go and get the coal from the cellar.
The water should soon be hot enough for a bath.

6 Sentence and full stop

As you can see, each sentence makes sense by itself, although the meaning connects it to the others. Here are three more groups of words, this time not sentences:

it was raining when
opened the window with a
must remember that it isn't

Now let us add other words in order to complete the sense:

It was raining when he arrived at the bridge.
She opened the window with a long pole.
You must remember that it isn't his bike.

These groups of words are now complete; they are sentences. Each one begins with a capital letter, and ends with a full stop.

Turn to Oral practice 1 and 2

Recognizing where sentences end

When you read a piece of English out loud, you pause at the end of each sentence. If you have written something yourself, read it aloud, noting where you make the longer pauses. This will help you decide where sentences end.

Turn to Oral practice 3, 4 and 5

Oral practice

1 Read through these word groups carefully, and then say which ones are sentences, making sense by themselves:

   a) yesterday I met my friends at the pool
   b) if he comes he will bring a
   c) seven wild geese flew over our heads
   d) no-one likes ice cream on his bacon and eggs
   e) when they told me the good news
   f) don't forget to bring your raincoat
   g) winter is very long in Sweden but
   h) ten pence will not buy many sweets nowadays
   i) the fox went hunting by moonlight
   j) as they came into the house

Sentence and full stop 7

2. This passage must be divided into sentences by putting in full stops and capital letters. Where should they go?

   Rafiq opened the parcel this morning it was very large and heavy his sister Shina watched him carefully she knew it was for his birthday she had watched Mushtaq wrap it up a few days before.

3. Which of the following word groups are complete sentences?
   When you have decided that, add words to complete the others. For example b) might become: "Bring the plastic watering can into the garden."

   a) When you have finished, take
   b) watering can into the garden
   c) I am very fond of painting
   d) only take medicine if you
   e) don't come in here
   f) because of my cold
   g) bring me the book please
   h) I would never have done it if
   i) the flowers need watering
   j) I wonder why I have to tell you the date so often

4. Read out this passage. Say when a full stop or capital letter is needed.

   the boys went up to the door of the house it was not quite closed and they wondered if someone had been there before them they went inside to look around the first thing that they noticed was the thickness of the dust everywhere after glancing round the kitchen they went into the passage and up the stairs there was a loud squeak at each step they took at the top they paused for a moment because Tom thought he heard a noise he opened the first door on the right and inside it they saw signs of recent occupation there were clothes on the floor and a couple of suitcases on the table by craning his neck out of the window Leroy was able to keep watch on the drive and front door

5. Read out this passage. Say when a punctuation mark is needed, and of what kind.

   The nurse came over to the patient and asked him why he was out in the hospital grounds the patient immediately ran off the nurse chased him through the flower beds and into the car park she eventually cornered him and asked if it was the operation that was worrying him he told her he didn't mind the operation so much as having to spend the next three weeks in bed

8 Sentence and full stop

Self-test

Write out the following passages, putting in the necessary full stops and capital letters.

1 I picked up my two heavy suitcases and with a grimace I walked on, feeling as though the last hundred yards would stretch my arms permanently beyond their normal length I did not have to run any more that was some consolation I heard a cry and looked round it was my polish acquaintance he started to shout at me

2 the new road will run just behind the garden no doubt it will take several months to complete and will cause a great deal of mess the mess is bearable the noise, on the other hand, cannot be ignored perhaps one gets used to it after all, some people live by a busy railway in any case it will be worth it in the end

3 the town is on a spit of land between the harbour and a beach the roads are incredibly narrow and chock-a-block with holiday-makers you can drive your car through during the summer, but only at five in the morning cornish pasties are sold some are a disgrace, containing potato and swede and nothing much else complaints are greeted with blank stares one can buy good pasties but they must be searched for I would like to go there again, but in winter

 *Answers on page 60*

Self-test answers

1 Napoleon   Sparta   Greece   Philadelphia   Denis   Honda
2 This   Mr Buxtable Harvard   MA   South America He
   Mondays

Capital letters

Quick reference

> A CAPITAL LETTER
>
> 1 *Begins a sentence*
>
>   Spring is late this year.
>
> 2 *Begins the name of a particular*
>
>   PERSON   Jennifer
>   PLACE   Iceland
>   or THING   Statue of Liberty
>
> 3 *Is used in abbreviations*
>
>   MB   (Bachelor of Medicine)
>   RAF (Royal Air Force)
>   LA   (Los Angeles)

Information

1. A capital letter begins a sentence:
   John came in. The dog barked. Out went John.

2. The first letter of a name is a capital letter.
   Your own name begins with a capital letter because it is the special name of one particular person – you. Similarly, other names of a particular person, place or thing begin with capital letters. Here are some of them, divided into groups.

A *Countries/languages/people*

England/English/Englishman   Scotland/Gaelic/Scot
Holland/Dutch/Dutchman   India/Urdu/Indian

10 Capital letters

B *Oceans/seas/lakes*

The Pacific
The Red Sea
Lake Windermere
The Indian Ocean

C *Places*

Fleet Street
Athens
Burnt Mill School
The Red Lion
Mars

D *Books/films/plays*

Great Expectations
The Pigman
A Midsummer Night's Dream
Chariots of Fire

E *Continents*

Asia
Africa
Europe
Australasia

F *Days/months*

Monday
Sunday
February
Good Friday

G *People*

Charlie Chaplin
President Reagan
Paul McCartney
Margaret Thatcher

Turn to Oral practice 1

Notice that a name of a particular person, place or thing begins with a capital, but the general name which applies to a group of them does not.

Cumbernauld	town	Buckingham Palace	royal residence
Japan	country	Concorde	aeroplane
The Queen's Head	public house		

Turn to Oral practice 2 and 3

3 Capitals are used for abbreviations, as in the following:

GB   (Great Britain)
IOU £1   (I owe you £1)
CSE   (Certificate of Secondary Education)
IRA   (Irish Republican Army)
CND   (Campaign for Nuclear Disarmament)
DIY   (Do It Yourself)
WRNS   (Women's Royal Naval Service)
SDP   (Social Democratic Party)
RSVP   (Repondez s'il vous plait) – It means, "Please reply".

| Capital letters | 11 |

Oral practice

1 Think of some additional words for each of the seven groups which you have just read. For example, you might include Mexico and France in group A.

2 One or more words in each of the groups below needs an initial capital letter. Which are they?

   a) home   abroad   iceland   ireland   island
   b) sea   lake   english channel   north sea
   c) lock   loch   loch lomond   waterfalls   victoria falls
   d) desert   sahara desert   salisbury plain
   e) hills   quantocks   ben nevis   mountain
   f) state   alaska   seaside   bognor regis
   g) swamp   nile delta   russia   low land
   h) country   yorkshire   province   district
   i) king   queen   william the conqueror   admiral nelson   sailors

3 Capital letters and full stops have been left out of this passage, which is adapted from *Movements in European History* by D. H. Lawrence. First read it aloud to get the sense. Then go through it again saying when a capital letter, or a full stop and capital letter, is needed.

gadhel was an ancient mythical hero of prehistoric europe about whom we know little save that he gave his name to a great race of people, the gadhels or gaels there are gaels today in great britain their language gaelic is spoken in scotland, ireland, wales and brittany it was once the language of all france in the south of gaul was the great port of massilia, now called marseilles it soon rose to importance and became the rival of superb carthage, that wonderful city of the phoeniceans in north africa opposite the toe of italy.

Self-test

1 Make a list of the words given here which should begin with capital letters:

   coast   cart   intention   napoleon   sparta   greece
   acrobat   tennis   nicety   philadelphia   oracle   coracle
   denis   motorbike   honda

12 Capital letters

2 Rewrite this passage with the necessary capital letters (ten are needed):

this time the cards were dealt by mr buxtable, watched by a research worker from harvard who had an ma in psychical research from a college in south america. he made copious notes as the group endeavoured to overcome the laws of probability, as they had done the previous three mondays.

 *Answers on page 8*

Self-test answers

1 The team's captain, Sarah Symes, is an outstanding performer. She is a talented player, a good leader and a likeable person. She knows when to urge her team on, when to praise them and when to reprimand them. In the match last Saturday, which was played against a strong side, Sarah led her players to victory.

As soon as he turned back to the window, she raised herself on one elbow and parted the bed curtains. She saw the ghost take some carpenter's tools from his pocket – a hammer, a file, a small saw. He began to work on the window sill, ripping out the woodwork below it. Just as he tore the last board loose, a torrent of golden ducats poured on to the floor in a clinking stream. The ghost squatted and pulled more coins, of gold and silver, from a hollow place in the wall. Then he began to put the coins in piles, counting, counting, in a hoarse voice.

2 Commas are appropriate after the following words:

  a) Tendring Road,
  b) cars, stamps,
  c) grandmother, me,
  d) cases, regulations,
  e) Mona, restless,
  f) toothbrush, paste,
  g) Alison, else,
  h) not, so,
  i) grandfather, seven,
  j) her, then, quieter,
  k) couple, quiet,

Comma

Quick reference

THE MAIN USES ARE:

1 *To mark a pause in a sentence*
   He is lost, I'm sorry to say.

2 *To divide items in a list*
   Bring your hat, coat, umbrella and gloves.

3 *To mark off part of a sentence*
   The house, so they tell me, is collapsing.

Information

The main uses:

1 *To make a sentence easier to read and understand*

   When you read out a passage of English you pause at the full stop which ends each sentence. You also make shorter pauses within each sentence to make the meaning clearer. These shorter pauses are marked by commas. For example:

   Remember, it's a long way.
   If the milkman comes, buy some cream.
   I didn't enjoy the book, but I'm not sure why.
   "Michael, bring some butter please."

   Turn to Oral practice 1 and 2

2 *In lists*

   When you write a list of short items, you should put a comma after each one, as in the following:

| 14 | Comma |

He carried a pen, several pencils, coloured paper, a rubber, six ball points, a pencil sharpener and a ruler.

Notice that there is no comma before the final *and*.

Turn to Oral practice 3

3 *In pairs*

Sometimes commas act as markers or brackets, marking off extra information in the middle of a sentence, as here:

I saw a fence, a relic of the old farm, blown down in the gale.

This is made up of two statements, (1) I saw the fence blown down in the gale. (2) (the fence was) a relic of the old farm. The second statement can be placed in the middle of the first, without confusion, by putting a comma before it and after it.

Turn to Oral practice 4

Oral practice

1 Read the sentences aloud and say where a comma is needed.
   a) If you go out take your coat with you.
   b) Look there's a path over there.
   c) When the bell rings bring the tea please.
   d) Although there was a shortage we always had plenty.
   e) Look under the bed behind the door and in the cupboard.
   f) She came but most reluctantly.
   g) Boys get a couple of footballs.

2 Read these sentences aloud, saying where commas are needed.
   a) I was late as you might well imagine.
   b) I don't think that was necessary do you?
   c) Mow the grass clean the windows and take the dog for a walk.
   d) Holders of green cards are allowed in the porter told me.
   e) So that we would believe him he showed us his passport.
   f) She brought her cat a creature I do not like.

3 Say where commas are needed in these sentences.
   a) The governors headmistress and staff invite you to the school sports.
   b) Open your books files brief cases or dispatch cases.

c) The packet contained black purple grey green and orange felt tips.
d) Books photographs paper maps and clothing were strewn all over the floor.
e) Wine spirits perfume cigarettes cigars and tobacco were all sold in the duty free shop.

4 A pair of commas would be appropriate in five of the following six sentences. Say where.

   a) The policeman hearing a strange noise rushed to investigate.
   b) Some people I must admit much prefer maths to English.
   c) Winter season of snow and ice is past.
   d) He jogged he asserted five miles at least.
   e) Dancing is one of my favourite pastimes.
   f) It is the right time of the year so I am told to plant tomatoes.

Self-test

1 Rewrite these passages adding commas where needed:

The team's captain Sarah Symes is an outstanding performer. She is a talented player a good leader and a likeable person. She knows when to urge her team on when to praise them and when to reprimand them. In the match last Saturday which was played against a strong side Sarah led her players to victory.

As soon as he turned back to the window she raised herself on one elbow and parted the bed curtains. She saw the ghost take some carpenter's tools from his pocket – a hammer a file a small saw. He began to work on the window sill ripping out the woodwork below it. Just as he tore the last board loose a torrent of golden ducats poured on to the floor in a clinking stream. The ghost squatted and pulled more coins of gold and silver from a hollow place in the wall. Then he began to put the coins in piles counting counting in a hoarse voice.

2 Each of the following sentences would be improved by the addition of one or more commas. Write them out, clearly punctuated.

   a) The coalman visited Tendring Road Sheering Avenue and New Street.
   b) His hobby is collecting old cars new stamps ginger jars and Wedgwood china.
   c) His grandmother they tell me is saintlike.

16 Comma

d) That's true in some cases according to the regulations but not in others.
e) Upstairs Mona restless murmurs and mutters in her sleep.
f) She has taken just a few personal things – toothbrush paste cleansing cream.
g) Alison like everyone else is wearing jeans and a tee-shirt.
h) You are not if you don't mind me saying so too good a knitter.
i) My grandfather who died recently at the age of eighty-seven was a life-long activist in his trade union.
j) The man watched her then when she was quieter he pulled her towards him and comforted her.
k) They forgot why the couple once so quiet had turned so nasty.

 *Answers on page 12*

Self test-answers

1		2			
1	?	a)	!!	f)	!!
2	!	b)	.	g)	?
3	.	c)	?	h)	!.
4	!	d)	?	i)	!?
5	!	e)	?	j)	?
6	.				
7	.				

Question mark
Exclamation mark

Quick reference

> EXAMPLES:
>
> What is the time?
> Do you know him?
> Who won?
>
> Each of these sentences asks a question. Therefore it ends in a question mark instead of a full stop.
>
> EXAMPLES:
>
> Keep the dog in!
> Just you wait!
> That's *my* idea!
>
> An exclamation mark tells you that the words are spoken with emotion or surprise. It replaces a full stop at the end of a sentence.

Information

A QUESTION MARK OR AN EXCLAMATION MARK IS USED INSTEAD OF A FULL STOP.

Question mark

The name "question mark" explains itself. Put it at the end of any sentence which asks a question.

The question may be short: Why?
                                        Why not?
                                        Who?
                                        What?

It may be long: If I eat the gooseberries before they are ripe, are you sure that I will get the tummy-ache?

– but in every case you need a question mark at the end.

Turn to Oral practice 1 and 2

Exclamation mark

An exclamation mark at the end of a sentence helps the reader to put the right stress, or feeling, into the words he or she reads. Often they have to be said with surprise or excitement, for example:

Don't shout!
John has broken three cups today!
Don't drink that – it's poison!
I never saw such an enormous cat in all my life!

Turn to Oral practice 3

Question and exclamation marks

If you write down what people are saying, you put the punctuation mark *before* the inverted commas. For example:

"Is this your boat?" he asked.
"No," replied the lion tamer. "I don't like water."
"Why not?"
"Well it makes me nervous. So there!"

Turn to Oral practice 4 and 5

An indirect question

An indirect question *tells* you that someone asked a question, but *does not ask it* directly. For example:

I asked her if she was ready for the gum-chewing race.
He was asked whether the money was still in the old sock.

Use a full stop at the end, *not* a question mark.

Turn to Oral practice 6

Question, exclamation mark 19

Oral practice

Question marks

1 Six of the following ten sentences need question marks. Which are they?

   a) What is the time
   b) Is it time you went to bed
   c) There is cake for supper
   d) He had done it, hadn't he
   e) Vanessa is nowhere to be found
   f) What does that mean
   g) He wonders what they are crying about
   h) Is that the absolute truth
   i) The fire engine is on its way
   j) Do you know what day it is

2 Make up five questions each beginning with one of the following:

   a) Who   b) What   c) Why   d) When   e) How

Exclamation marks

3 Which of these sentences could end with an exclamation mark?

   a) Look out
   b) Have a cup of tea, Peter
   c) What a beautiful coin
   d) I've had my tea, thanks
   e) I wonder what the time is
   f) Don't drop that vase
   g) There is the toy shop
   h) I like a quiet evening by the fire
   i) Fire
   j) He's killed the general

Question marks and exclamation marks

4 What punctuation mark is needed to replace each of the numbers below: full stop, exclamation mark or question mark?

   a) I wonder what the jungle is like (1)
   b) Do you ever wonder what the moon is made of (2)
   c) It is absolutely green (3) Is it really (4)
   d) He has done nothing that you asked him to do (5)
   e) Good heavens, he is nowhere to be found (6)
   f) Ask her where the money is coming from (7)
   g) "What is all this about (8)" asked the lion tamer (9)
   h) "Help (10) help (11) help (12)' came the cry from the cage (13)
   i) "Why do some buses have a half top deck (14)" asked Janie (15)

| 20 | Question, exclamation mark |

5 Say what punctuation marks should replace each number in these sentences.
   a) Where have you put my cup (1) Give it to me this instant (2)
   b) "One woman, one vote (3) One woman, one vote (4)" they yelled as they marched down the street.
   c) Where is the painting by Picasso that Auntie gave you for Christmas (5)
   d) It is made of ivory, isn't it (6)

6 Make up five questions, changing each in turn into an indirect question. Here is an example:

"Has the dog come in?"
Mother asked me whether the dog had come in.

Self-test

1 Write down the numbers which are in the brackets below, and against each one write the punctuation mark which should replace it.
   a) Where is Paul (1) Tell me at once (2)
   b) Ask the waiter where he has hidden the tea cosy (3)
   c) "Jobs for all (4) Jobs for all (5)" he shouted at the meeting (6)
   d) Peter asked Dawn where the nest was (7)

2 Replace the asterisks with an exclamation mark or question mark or full stop.
   a) Beware* It's going to explode*
   b) I wonder whether she's as strong as she says she is*
   c) Do you know if she's as strong as she claims to be*
   d) Where can I find the answer to this problem*
   e) Which days of the week do you receive a delivery*
   f) It *can't* be true* What an amazing stroke of luck*
   g) Why have they boycotted the Olympics*
   h) Well done* That really is an achievement*
   i) What a shame* There's no justice in this world is there*
   j) How are we ever to achieve peace when politicians behave like that*

   *Answers on page 16*

Question, exclamation mark

Self-test answers

1. a) Rosen's b) car's c) women's, men's d) day's e) anyone's
   f) Stephen's g) Martin's h) Davies' i) court's, tribunal's
   j) Babies' k) school's, pupils'

2. The boy's coat was on the gerbils' cage. They were hiding in the tree's shade; perhaps because they disliked the garment's smoke-laden smell. A couple of naturalists looked out from the neighbours' doorway.

Apostrophe 1

The use of the apostrophe to show possession or relationship.

Quick reference

1 An apostrophe replaces the word "of".

The friend of Angela *becomes* Angela's friend
The travel card of the student *becomes* The student's travel card

2 If the word is plural ending in "s" the apostrophe comes last.

The armoured-car of the soldiers
becomes
The soldiers' armoured-car

BUT Plurals formed without an "s" do this:

Women – the women's team
Children – the children's competition

Information

First, here are two examples:

The bone of the dog – the dog's bone
The milk of the cat – the cat's milk

We have used an apostrophe in *dog's* and *cat's* to show that something belongs to them. Here are three more examples:

My friend's coat
Mandy's cat
Dad's old car

Turn to Oral practice 1

If the word is simply plural (more than one) you don't need an apostrophe. For example:

That company makes toys.
Apprentices need caring managers.

Turn to Oral practice 2

Look at the above examples again. Note that the apostrophe goes in front of the final "s" – friend's, Mandy's, Dad's. This is because there is *one* friend, *one* Mandy, *one* Dad. They are singular words.

Plurals ending in "s"

If the words are plural (more than one), the apostrophe goes after the "s":
the cafe of the students – the students' cafe
the books of the pupils – the pupils' books
a nest of ants – an ants' nest

Turn to Oral practice 3

Plurals without a final "s"

The plural of *man* is *men*; the plural of *child* is *children*. With such words we add apostrophes ('s) as for singulars.

men's shirts
the children's playgroup

Turn to Oral practice 4

Relationships

Note that the apostrophe used in this way may express a relationship which is not really possessive. If we say *John's uncle* we do not mean John owns his uncle. In fact many different relationships are expressed by *of the* or by an apostrophe. E.g. in one week's time.

A name ending in "s"

If a name already ends in "s" we need not add a second "s", e.g.

Hercules   Mr Peters   John Keats

Hercules' tomb   Mr Peters' shop   John Keats' cottage

Rule of thumb: if you pronounce the additional "s" when speaking, add it when writing. *Mrs Jones's sports car.*

| 24 | Apostrophe 1 |

Oral practice

1 One word in each of these sentences needs an apostrophe. Say which.

   a) He met his mothers friend.
   b) The books last page is missing.
   c) Where is Sonyas pair of skates?
   d) He says he likes his brothers picture best.
   e) The benchs legs are wobbly.
   f) The captains table is always stable.

2 Say which word needs the apostrophe in each pair of sentences and explain why.

   a) The cats are howling. The cats dinner is ready.
   b) There are five soldiers outside. That is the soldiers bayonet.
   c) They are eating their daughters cake. Martin has two young daughters.
   d) Who broke the carpenters vice? Several carpenters are waiting outside.
   e) They like fast cars. That cars exhaust is trailing on the ground.
   f) All the trains are late. That trains driver is standing outside.

3 Read these out, replacing "of" or "of the" by an apostrophe. Say where the apostrophe goes.

   a) the climax of the play
   b) the scent of flowers
   c) the friend of my brother
   d) the hooters of ships
   e) the fishing rod of the sailor
   f) the green eye of the little yellow god
   g) the hideout of the bandit
   h) the barracks of the Coldstream Guards

4 In the following passage there are ten words which require an apostrophe. Say which they are.

The childrens uncle and Annes father met to discuss their plans for the holiday. The adults could not agree because ones idea was to have a restful time while the others intention was to go out and climb mountain peaks. The meetings result was that the first weeks holiday would be spent by the sea and the last weeks holiday would be in North Wales. They estimated both cars capacity very carefully, so that they would be able to limit their luggage to what they could carry.

"My friends luggage trailer would be very useful," said Anne. "It would easily hold all uncles camping gear."

Self-test

1. Write out the words needing apostrophes.

   a) We enjoyed reading Michael Rosens poems.
   b) The cars brakes must all be examined.
   c) Womens clothes cost more than mens.
   d) The next camp was a days walk away.
   e) My brother cooks all the meals in our house – unfortunately without reference to anyones tastes.
   f) What do we commemorate on St Stephens Day?
   g) Martins sports car was the talk of the neighbourhood.
   h) Mrs Davies business contacts extend all over the world.
   i) Union officials disrupted the courts verdict and asked for the tribunals decision to be reversed.
   j) Babies early speech patterns are fascinating to study.
   k) The schools reputation was damaged by the pupils decision to go on strike.

2. Rewrite this passage with an apostrophe (correctly placed) to replace "of the" where possible. The passage will begin: *"The boy's coat –*

   The coat of the boy was on the cage of the gerbils. The gerbils were hiding in the shade of the tree; perhaps because they disliked the smoke-laden smell of the garment. A couple of naturalists looked out from the doorway of the neighbours.

Answers on page 21

Self-test answers

1. a) shouldn't b) we've, didn't c) Hole's d) they've e) you're
   f) aren't g) let's h) you're i) it's

2. a) he isn't or he's not b) I'm sure c) That can't be d) We're watching e) Father's seen it. f) you're g) I'll h) Where's

3. a) That is b) you have c) he cannot d) Who has e) Who is f) she is g) it is h) mother is i) they are

4. a) there b) their c) it's d) its e) who's f) whose

5. a) they're b) there, their c) It's d) its e) whose f) who's

Apostrophe 2

The use of the apostrophe to show letters left out.

Quick reference

> When we talk we often save time by running two words together.
>
> In writing we do the same, and we mark it with an apostrophe:
>
> | | | |
> |---|---|---|
> | I am sure | becomes | I'm sure |
> | It was not ready | becomes | It wasn't ready |
> | Rita has won! | becomes | Rita's won! |
> | It is just not fair | becomes | It's just not fair |

Information

We can use the apostrophe to shorten a word. Thus,
I do not like apples can be shortened to *I don't like apples*.
We have taken the letter *o* out of the word *not* and put in an apostrophe, making *don't*. Here are other examples:

He has not	he hasn't
I was not	I wasn't
I am surprised	I'm surprised

Sometimes we leave several letters out:

They cannot	they can't
I shall not	I shan't

Turn to Oral practice 1 and 2

When talking to each other we make the words flow more rapidly by running two words together and shortening them, e.g. *wasn't, you're, won't, can't*. When we write them down, we put an apostrophe in where we take letters out; this makes it clear to the reader that the words are shortened. Often the shorter form sounds more natural than the longer.

Thus, *"I cannot help it"* sounds rather awkward. We would normally say *"I can't help it"*.

Turn to Oral practice 3 and 4

Some words have the same sound, but different meanings. We don't get confused when we hear them, because the sense is obvious. For example:

Here comes the *train*.
Athletes must *train* regularly.

Here are some common examples which involve the apostrophe.

1 There – their – they're

There often has to do with a place as in here and there, it's over there, we've been there; it is also used in sentences like There will be rain tomorrow. There are too many for me to handle. There was no room in the hotel.

Their is the plural of his, her and its; it means of them or belonging to them. For example: They ate their sandwiches on the beach.

They're is a shortened form of they are; the apostrophe (') shows that the letter a has been omitted. For example: Look out, they're coming. They're in the playing field.

Turn to Oral practice 5

2 Its – it's

Its means *of it*. Instead of saying "The cat fell on the cat's feet", you would say (or write) "The cat fell on *its* feet"; the *its* shows possession or belonging.

It's is short for *it is* or *it has*. The apostrophe (') shows that *"i"* or *"ha"* has been missed out. For example: It's going to rain. (= it *is*). It's been a very cold winter. (= it *has*)

Turn to Oral practice 6

3 Your – you're

Your means *belonging to* as in "You will break your leg if you do that". *You're* is short for *you are* and the apostrophe shows that the "a" has been omitted. For example: You're very tall for your age.

Turn to Oral practice 7

4 Who's – whose

Who's is short for *who is* or *who has*. Whenever *who's* is used at the start of a sentence, remember to put a question mark at the end. The apostrophe shows that a letter or letters have been omitted.

e.g. *Who's* the lucky-number winner?
Who's played this game before?

Or it can be used in the middle of a sentence:

I recognize the girl *who's* just entered the room.
Do you know anything about the manageress *who's* just been appointed?

Whose is used to show possession:

e.g. The woman *whose* house we are in is unknown to all the guests.
The TV star *whose* picture is on that magazine cover died yesterday in mysterious circumstances.

Turn to Oral practice 8

Oral practice

1 What are the shortened forms of each of the following? Where would you put an apostrophe? The first one is done for you.

a) he has not (he hasn't)   d) I am late   g) he does not
b) you have not   e) you are on time   h) they will not
c) they did not   f) he is cold   i) they are late

2 Read this passage aloud. Then go through it again saying which words need an apostrophe and where it should go.

They werent ready because they hadnt been told that the clock wasnt keeping good time and so I shant complain that Ive been obliged to wait for hours.

3 Read out this passage, expanding the shortened words to full length. The first one is done for you.

I won't (= will not) say we've never guessed where Jack's hiding his treasure, but I've no idea where he'll put it when Bill's solved the secret. The last thing he said to me before his journey was, "Bill shan't have it. I'll make sure he'll look in the wrong places. It ain't fair, because he'd be richer than all of us if he got the treasure."

Apostrophe 2   29

(One of the shortened double words in this passage is slang – which one?)

4 Read out these sentences as they stand. Then read them again running two words together where possible. Say where the apostrophe would go.

    a) I am surprised that you are so late.
    b) We are not coming until you have finished the washing up.
    c) They are ready.
    d) Who is eating what is intended for the cat?
    e) Where is the cake Jake has made?

5 Read out these sentences, spelling out *there*, *their*, *they're*, whichever is needed:

    a) It's over ..... by the piano.
    b) ..... clothes were soaked by rain.
    c) If ..... coming in, I'm leaving.
    d) ..... going to miss ..... train.
    e) ..... is no chance of my borrowing ..... house while ..... away.

6 Say which is correct in each of these sentences, *its* or *it's:*

    a) The dog hurt ..... leg.
    b) ..... getting darker every minute.
    c) ..... been a long time since I last saw you.
    d) ..... about time that dog went into ..... kennel.
    e) .... own fault if it gets in the way.

7 Use *your* or *you're* to fill in the blanks, spelling out the one you choose.

    a) ..... not disturbing me at all.
    b) Have you finished ..... soup?
    c) ..... not using ..... experience.
    d) ..... main fault is that ..... too lazy.

8 Use *whose* or *who's* to fill in the blanks, spelling out the one you choose.

    a) ..... taken my place in the team?
    b) This is my aunt ..... looking after me.
    c) We've traced the gentleman ..... umbrella you took.
    d) ..... going to say ..... captain?
    e) Now tell me again, ... trespassing on ..... land?

Apostrophe 2

Self-test

1. Write out any words which need an apostrophe.

   a) It shouldnt cost too much.
   b) Weve eaten the food he didnt pay for.
   c) A Black Holes not easy for laymen to understand.
   d) Theyve argued that such things exist.
   e) They attract the people youre thinking of.
   f) There just arent enough reasonable jobs these days, even for the well-qualified.
   g) Lets consider taking a holiday abroad this year.
   h) Youre unlikely to find a cheaper flat to rent than this one.
   i) Its pointless worrying over something which happened so long ago.

2. Rewrite these phrases, using an apostrophe in each one and leaving out letters where necessary.

   a) He is not.
   b) I am sure.
   c) That cannot be.
   d) We are watching.
   e) Father has seen it.
   f) You are going to get into trouble.
   g) I shall be honest with you.
   h) Where is the key?

3. Write each of these shortened forms in full.

   a) That's true.
   b) You've succeeded.
   c) He can't swim.
   d) Who's been here?
   e) Who's afraid?
   f) She's lying.
   g) It's just not true.
   h) Mother's crying again.
   i) They're always arguing.

4. Fill in the gaps in these sentences with the appropriate word from the right hand side of the page.

   a) ..... are seven altogether.
   b) They took ..... friends with them.   } their, they're, there
   c) ..... a long way to Colchester on foot.
   d) He saw the lion cub run to ..... mother.   } it's, its

e) Do you know ..... coming? } whose, who's
f) I wonder ..... musical box that is.

5 Say which word should fill each gap:

a) ..... coming when they can.
b) I saw them over ....., sailing ..... yacht. } their, they're, there
c) ..... not true.
d) The box fell on to ..... side. } its, it's
e) ..... is that?
f) ..... that? } whose, who's

 *Answers on page 25*

Self-test answers

1 a) "I think the tea is cold," he said.
   b) "The cold weather is early this winter, don't you think?" asked the gasman.
   c) "I am not surprised," said Mr Bates. "I am not surprised at all."
   d) Angelo smiled. "You will get used to the heat in time," he said.
   e) "I reckon he's dead," said the nurse.
   f) "Where did you get to the other evening?" Dan asked his mates.
   g) "The chances of a nuclear holocaust," began the professor, "are growing daily."
   h) "Why," shouted the defendant, "will no-one listen to what I have to say?"
   i) "The public have been marvellous in their help," commented the spokeswoman.
   j) "I feel very honoured to receive this award on behalf of my mother," the actress announced. "Our family will always treasure it."
   k) "There can be little doubt in my mind," the director concluded, "that we have found the perfect actor for the lead rôle."

2 (Alternatives are in brackets)

   The professor returned to the lecture room almost as soon as he had left it. "I suppose," he said, "You've none of you noticed my glasses. (?)" Everyone began to look on and around and under the table (,) but without result. "Does anyone remember if I had them on?" Heads nodded affirmatively. "I must have (,) or I wouldn't have been able to read the documents we studied."

   "Are they in your pocket?" was the suggestion of one student.

   "That's it. (!) That's it. (!)" He produced the spectacles. "Thank you so much."

Speech marks: inverted commas

Quick reference

SPEECH MARKS ENCLOSE WORDS SPOKEN

"You'll find the factory down the next street."

ANYTHING ELSE IS OUTSIDE THE SPEECH MARKS

The stranger said, "You'll find the factory down the next street." I thanked him and walked on.

Note Books, magazines and newspapers often use 'single' instead of "double" inverted commas.

Information

We put inverted commas before and after the words spoken:
   "That's my house," the boy told me.
   His answer was, "Ice cream is cheap."

Turn to Oral practice 1 and 2

The purpose of inverted commas

When writing a story, or an account of an event, we may want the reader to know the actual words that a person said. To do this we enclose them in inverted commas. Sometimes pairs of inverted commas have to be used twice in one sentence. Here is an example:

First pair   **Second pair**

"I saw him once," said the sheriff, "but I don't remember where it was."

Speech marks

The words *said the sheriff* were not spoken and so cannot go inside inverted commas.

Turn to Oral practice 3 and 4

Here are the rules:

1. Inverted commas go before and after the words spoken:
   "Give it up!" they cried.

2. Use a comma instead of a full stop if the sentence continues after the inverted commas.
   "They make clothes here," said the night watchman.

   But exclamation marks remain unchanged:
   "Stand up!" said Fred.

3. Other punctuation marks go inside inverted commas:
   "Bring a chair," mother called.
   "Is it true?" Peter asked.

4. Wherever the spoken sentence comes, it begins with a capital letter, even after a comma.
   I told him, "The door is open."

5. When writing a conversation between two or more people, put each new speaker on a new line, and begin away from the margin:
   "Do you come here often?" he asked.
   "Only when I have to, but that may be several times a week," I replied sadly.
   "Well, well," he said. "I don't envy you. I always find it very cold and bleak, especially when it snows."
   "It's not as bad as all that," Julie interrupted.

Turn to Oral practice 5

Oral practice

1. Read out the words actually spoken in each of these sentences:

   a) "That's my hat," said the girl.
   b) "Food is very expensive," said mother.
   c) "Come here!" the policewoman shouted. "The ambulance can't wait!"
   d) "I do not," said Geoffrey, "eat overripe plums."

34 Speech marks

2. Where are inverted commas needed in these sentences?

   a) The table needs laying said my sister.
   b) Do you like cheese? she asked.
   c) The security guard said, London is more dangerous than other cities.
   d) Come here! was the cry.
   e) The dog-lover whispered, he doesn't look harmless and I don't trust him.

3. Which words are actually spoken in these sentences? The first is done for you.

   a) Pass the spanner, called the mechanic. ("Pass the spanner.")
   b) Have you seen this person, asked the policeman, holding up a photograph.
   c) What do you want to go there for, demanded Aunt Angela, if you don't know what it's like?
   d) First take the tiller in your right hand, said the instructor, and then pull in the main sheet.
   e) If you haven't got a map or a compass, said the leader, we'd better lend you ours, or you won't find your way.
   f) I take the exam next Monday, said Paul, and I haven't even started my revision.

4. Read these sentences aloud; then read them again, saying where inverted commas and other punctuation marks are needed.

   a) Is this the road to the sea asked the motorist.
   b) I don't know replied the pedestrian I'm a stranger here myself.
   c) Why isn't there a signpost I wonder sighed the motorist.
   d) I told you you should have bought a map said his wife and now it's too late because the shops are shut.
   e) I know said her husband becoming rather angry I did think that even though we are in the wilds there might be such things as signposts.

5. Read through this passage twice, the second time saying where inverted commas are needed.

   Where on earth have you put the new inner tube for my bike? shouted Andrew in an angry voice. You know I've got to fit it on before the trip tomorrow. He rummaged furiously through the cupboard under the stairs. I bet you've moved it, he said. I'm sure you have. It's your mania for clearing up. He glared ferociously at his elder sister, who looked indifferent.

Speech marks

Self-test

1 Rewrite these sentences properly punctuated:

   a) I think the tea is cold he said
   b) The cold weather is early this winter don't you think asked the gasman
   c) I am not surprised said Mr Bates I am not surprised at all
   d) Angelo smiled you will get used to the heat in time he said
   e) I reckon he's dead said the nurse
   f) Where did you get to the other evening Dan asked his mates
   g) The chances of a nuclear holocaust began the professor are growing daily
   h) Why shouted the defendant will no-one listen to what I have to say
   i) The public have been marvellous in their help commented the spokesman
   j) I feel very honoured to receive this award on behalf of my mother the actress announced Our family will always treasure it
   k) There can be little doubt in my mind the director concluded that we have found the perfect actor for the lead rôle

2 Punctuate the following passage and set it out correctly:

The professor returned to the lecture room almost as soon as he had left it i suppose he said youve none of you noticed my glasses everyone began to look on and around and under the table but without result does anyone remember if i had them on heads nodded affirmatively i must have or i wouldnt have been able to read the documents we studied are they in your pocket was the suggestion of one student thats it thats it he produced the spectacles thank you so much.

 *Answers on page 31*

Note

Inverted commas are also used to indicate the *title* of something – for example:

Have you read "Come to Mecca" by Farrukh Dhondy?
My favourite novel is "The Day of the Jackal".
Which film did you like best – "Superman 1" or "Superman 2"?

Speech marks

Self-test answers

1 (the 2.30 p.m.)   (the 3.00 p.m.)   (the 4.30 p.m.)

2 a) The Royal Institute of British Architects (RIBA for short) is based in London.
   b) No-one (so my sister asserted) is properly dressed.
   c) Four coal mines (two in Scotland and two in Wales) were obliged to close.
   d) The biggest state (Texas) elects two senators; so do the small ones (Rhode Island; Connecticut).
   e) Write the identifying letters (A to E) on a postcard and add the name of the pop star you think each photo represents.
   f) The Prime Minister (pictured left) was on a tour of the West Midlands yesterday.
   g) "Play for Today" (BBC 1, 9.30) is written by the celebrated novelist, Graham Greene.
   h) In Parliament today David Alton (Con. Solihull) condemned the latest wave of football hooliganism.
   i) We took the bus to the seaside resort of Ricisce for twenty dinars (twenty-five pence).
   j) My mother was (still is) enthusiastic about my sister's new job, but thinks she will have problems settling into an all-male assembly line.
   k) He was a real outsider (ate snails, it was said) and his strange morning rituals amazed us.

Brackets

Quick reference

> Brackets are also known as parentheses.
> You can add a word or phrase to a sentence by putting it inside brackets (like this).
>
> EXAMPLES:
>
> His brother (the silent one) enjoys reading. The horse ran today (Newmarket 3.30 p.m.) and won by three lengths.
>
> USE BRACKETS SPARINGLY

Information

Brackets (these things) are a way of enclosing one statement inside another, for example:

My uncle Arthur is a great favourite of mine. My uncle Arthur owns a pub.

can become:

My uncle Arthur (the pub owner) is a great favourite of mine.

This is presenting the same information in just one sentence, and in a more concise way than in the two separate statements.

Turn to Oral practice 1

Brackets can also be used to define, or explain further, something just mentioned, for example:

Having shared in both his father's passion (fishing) and his mother's (sailing) he was naturally delighted to live by the sea.
Philately (stamp collecting) and campanology (bell ringing) were his two great interests.

Turn to Oral practice 2

38 Brackets

Often we can use either brackets or commas. For example:

Esther (her best friend) ignored Sharon in the street.
Esther, her best friend, ignored Sharon in the street.

Oral practice

1 Where could you put brackets in these sentences?

   a) The steeplejack there's an unenviable job for you is at least his own boss when he is working.
   b) This generous man no-one can deny that he *was* generous was also extremely careful to invest his money wisely.
   c) She left all her money what was left of it that is to her housekeeper, none at all to her husband and children.
   d) You can use a cigar box provided you manage to find one to make a simple musical instrument.

2 Read out the words which could go inside brackets:

   a) Lai Hon bless her heart has given me a pair of slippers for my birthday.
   b) Ornithology bird watching was something that gave him endless pleasure.
   c) The story of the murder horribly exaggerated appeared in the following morning's papers.
   d) Alan Howard Henry VI and Charlotte Cornwell Queen Margaret were well cast in Shakespeare's *Henry VI*.
   e) St Albans Verulamium and York Eboracum were two of many towns established by the Romans during their occupation of Britain.

Self-test

1 The following passage is adapted from a racing report in a newspaper. Rewrite it using three pairs of brackets.

   John Carrington is the trainer worth following at Aintree today with Golden Boy the 2.30 p.m., Peter's Trap the 3.00 p.m. and Davey Lad the 4.30 p.m.

Brackets 39

2 Write down the phrases which can go inside brackets.

a) The Royal Institute of British Architects RIBA for short is based in London.
b) No-one so my sister asserted is properly dressed.
c) Four coal mines two in Scotland and two in Wales were obliged to close.
d) The biggest state Texas elects two senators; so do the small ones Rhode Island; Connecticut.
e) Write the identifying letters A to E on a postcard and add the name of the pop star you think each photo represents.
f) The Prime Minister pictured left was on a tour of the West Midlands yesterday.
g) "Play for Today" BBC 1, 9.30 is written by the celebrated novelist, Graham Greene.
h) In Parliament today David Alton Con. Solihull condemned the latest wave of football hooliganism.
i) We took the bus to the seaside resort of Ricisce for twenty dinars twenty-five pence.
j) My mother was still is enthusiastic about my sister's new job, but thinks she will have problems settling into an all-male assembly line.
k) He was a real outsider ate snails, it was said and his strange morning rituals amazed us.

Answers on page 36

3 Write five sentences of your own, using brackets in each.

4 Brackets are also used widely by playwrights. Look at the following extracts from *My Sister's Eighteenth* a play by John McGrath.* You will notice that brackets are placed around stage directions or around words that help the actors and actresses to perform.

(**Mandy** *has run on to the stage. As* **Arnie** *grabs* **William** *by the throat with one hand, still holding* **Michelle** *by the other, she raises the guitar above his head*)

* *Studio Scripts: Power*, (Hutchinson)

Mandy: You let him go! Let go of both of them or I'll smash this guitar. All over your head. . . .

William: You won't get away with this, you know, I'll have your engagement cancelled –

Michelle: (*Giving up biting the hand that holds her wrist*) Smash it, Mandy!

Barrie: (*Jumping on to the stage*) You put a scratch on that, and I'll ram your teeth so far down your throat your fillings'll fall out every time you sit down –

Mandy: One step closer and it goes into the drum-kit!

(**Susan** *comes in. Looks around in surprise*)

Susan: William – what is this? Party-games?

William: Well, it's a sort of trial of strength actually. These two friends of mine were not doing anybody any harm, but this ape-man here thinks he's big, strong and stupid and can push them around.

Arnie: (*To* **Barrie**) That's her, the fancy tut.

Barrie: (*To* **Susan**, *smiles*) Hello – I'm Barrie.

Self-test answers

1. a) I stocked up for the winter with essentials: moth balls, aniseed balls, chocolate tea cakes and sea cucumbers.
   b) They asked me what the words above the door could mean: "Abandon hope all ye who enter here."
   c) His record sheet reads as follows: "This man has failed dismally in everything except making money."
   d) The gist of his argument was this: there's no business like show business.
   e) Four cinemas have changed into Bingo Halls: The Odeon, ABC, Majestic and Grand.
   f) Please bring the things we need: axe, ropes, saw and safety helmets.
   g) Her answer surprised me: "Eat them yourself."
   h) You must see all the famous sights of America: The Grand Canyon, The Statue of Liberty, Cape Kennedy and my aunt's performing seal.
   i) The builders will need various materials: three bags of cement; a small quantity of sand; tiles and some extra copper piping.

Colon

Quick reference

The two main uses are:

1 To begin a list.

   These are all Scottish names: Ian, Alistair, Morag and Hamish.

2 To mark the beginning of an explanation of what has just been said.

   I heard a nasty noise: the sound of the exhaust bumping along the road.

Information

The colon is a punctuation mark. It looks like a double-decker full stop. It is used to begin a list of items –

They took everything they needed for camping: a tent, sleeping bags, airbeds, a water carrier and a dozen other things.

Turn to Oral practice 1 and 2

There is a second and similar use of the colon. When a word or phrase is explained or expanded later in the sentence it may be followed by a colon. Here is an example with the word or phrase underlined:

He told me the <u>cause of the accident</u>: the chimney had fallen through the roof during the recent gales.

Notice that the colon marks a natural pause: that is, if you were reading something aloud, you would pause there. It is used only when there is such a pause.

Turn to Oral practice 3 and 4

Colon

Oral practice

Each of the following sentences contains a list and requires a colon. Read them out, saying where a colon should go.

1. a) He carried all the luggage three suitcases, four paper parcels, a doll and a yapping poodle.
   b) My brother is good at cooking sweet things puddings, cakes, tarts, biscuits and trifle.
   c) There were only a few pieces of equipment in the store three long counters, five stools, a cash register and a washing-up machine.
   d) A soldier must be prepared to face all kinds of danger aerial attack, guerrilla warfare, rockets, guided missiles and other things yet to be invented.

2. Make up three sentences, each including a colon and a list.
   Here is a possible beginning for the first one –

   English woodlands contain several species of tree:

3. Where would you put a colon in each of these sentences?

   a) He is eccentric and has a strange belief about the shape of the earth neither flat nor round but very similar to a rugby ball.
   b) The scientists are looking for a special dye one that will resist prolonged exposure to all the elements without fading.
   c) The result was what we had hoped for a pleasant holiday with plenty of sunshine.
   d) He told them the truth he intends to convert the barn into a nightclub.

4. Make three sentences in each of which a word or phrase *before* the colon is expanded or explained in the words *after* it. Here is an example:

   Kate revealed to them the news: their father was still climbing mountains in the Himalayas.

Self-test

1. Rewrite these sentences, using a colon in each one, and add any other punctuation needed:

Colon 43

a) I stocked up for the winter with essentials moth balls aniseed balls chocolate tea cakes and sea cucumbers
b) They asked me what the words above the door could mean Abandon hope all ye who enter here
c) His record sheet reads as follows this man has failed dismally in everything except making money
d) The gist of his argument was this theres no business like show business
e) Four cinemas have changed into Bingo Halls the odeon abc majestic and grand
f) Please bring the things we need axe ropes saw and safety helmets
g) Her answer surprised me eat them yourself
h) You must see all the famous sights of america the grand canyon the statue of liberty, cape kennedy and my aunts performing seal
i) The builders will need various materials three bags of cement a small quantity of sand tiles and some extra copper piping

Answers on page 40

Self-test answers

1 a) I can't find him; he must have gone.
   b) That isn't true; you don't know what happened.
   c) They looked very tired; they looked hungry too.
   d) The policewoman arrived; she was accompanied by two social workers.

2 a) Winter is here; the warm weather is behind us.
   b) No-one has yet visited the fun fair.
   c) It isn't here; perhaps she ate it.
   d) These cost you nothing; those are expensive.
   e) Gorillas are popular with children; children are sometimes popular with gorillas.
   (If you put a punctuation mark after 'zoos' in (f), it would be a comma.)
   g) The White House's main priority is to repair the damage to its relations with Latin America; it regards the present European attitude with concern.
   h) Several patients were affected by the dispute; a hospital spokesman offered no comment.
   i) The kidney transplant was, according to the surgeon, one of the most difficult operations she had ever performed.
   j) The jury passed sentence; the defendant passed out.

Semi-colon

Quick reference

A semi-colon has two main functions:

1. To act as a light-weight full stop:

    She was in love with Llanfairfechan; he couldn't even pronounce it.
    This is your bike; that is mine.

2. To separate longish items in a list:

    He complained about the lateness of the trains; the dirty carriages; the ill-lit waiting room; the lack of porters, and the staleness of buffet sandwiches.

NOTE THE FINAL COMMA (NOT SEMI-COLON)

Information

A semi-colon is a punctuation mark; it looks like a full stop over a comma.

First use

We can use it in place of a full stop, if the pause is less definite. Here are two examples:

Don't forget to give John his present; he is waiting for it.
Some people like roast beef; others prefer lamb.

In both cases a full stop would be correct, but a semi-colon makes the pause less marked. You can think of it as a light-weight full stop.

Semi-colon 45

Second use

When we are writing down a list, and each item in the list is several words long, we can separate them by semi-colons. Here is an example:

The results of the long hot summer were not all pleasant: trees dying in the woods and parks; a shortage of water, especially in Wales; forest fires in several areas; a severe strain on the fire service, and the drying up of rivers.

Notice that the list begins with a colon and that the final two items are separated by a *comma*, and not a semi-colon.

Oral practice

1 Five of the following seven sentences may be punctuated by a semi-colon acting as a light-weight full stop. Read them out, indicating where the semi-colons should go.

   a) Dave is here Junior is next door.
   b) Bring your dog today bring your other pets tomorrow.
   c) Don't forget the cymbals we need them now.
   d) The two ladies came to the stall but didn't buy anything.
   e) I asked him his name he didn't reply.
   f) She told me the whole story it took about an hour.
   g) That surprises me because the ropes were new.

2 Make up three sentences, in each of which a semi-colon is used as a light-weight full stop.

3 Read this sentence twice: the first time getting the sense, and the second time saying where the semi-colons should go.

   Nobody knew how long the work would take: choosing the wood carefully cutting it to requisite sizes buying the other furnishing materials assembling the wardrobe and last of all painting it.

   (NB a single comma is needed after *wardrobe*.)

4 Make up two extended lists, with the items separated by semi-colons. Here is a possible opening for one of them:

   He invented several remarkable gadgets that no-one had any use for:

Semi-colon

Self-test

1 Rewrite these sentences properly punctuated; use a semi-colon in each one.

    a) i cant find him he must have gone
    b) that isnt true you dont know what happened
    c) they looked very tired they looked hungry too
    d) the policewoman arrived she was accompanied by two social workers

2 Seven of these ten sentences need semi-colons. Write out all ten – adding any other punctuation needed.

    a) winter is here the warm weather is behind us
    b) no-one has yet visited the fun fair
    c) it isnt here perhaps she ate it
    d) these cost you nothing those are expensive
    e) gorillas are popular with children children are sometimes popular with gorillas
    f) chimpanzees are popular in zoos but not in suburban housing estates
    g) the white house's main priority is to repair the damage to its relations with latin america it regards the present european attitude with concern
    h) several patients were affected by the dispute a hospital spokeswoman offered no comment
    i) the kidney transplant was according to the surgeon one of the most difficult operations she had ever performed
    j) the jury passed sentence the defendant passed out

Answers on page 43

Self-test answers

The dash goes between these words:

a) Martha – what
b) here – no
c) back – don't; shan't – before
d) return – says
e) empty – guests
f) hacienda – a

Dash

Quick reference

A dash indicates a break in the sense, acting rather like a comma.

Stella rushed in – and rushed out again.
The meal – an open air barbecue – was delicious.

Occasionally it links two sentences together.

"Don't run – I've found it."

Dashes are common in letters and informal writing.
Use them sparingly in more formal work.

Note: In print a dash – is longer than a hyphen - !

Information

The dash is used when there is a break in the sentence, but little if any pause:

He may turn out to be a criminal – one of the those bank robbers you read about.

It is more often used in informal writing (say, a diary, or a letter to a friend, or the record of a conversation) than in formal writing.
For example:

We're in a hotel for a bit – probably shall look for a house for the winter here.

Turn to Oral practice 1

There are no hard and fast rules about using the dash. Instead you must be guided by usage (i.e. what is normally done). Do not use dashes frequently;

avoid them in examinations unless you are confident you can use them properly.

Occasionally two dashes are used like a pair of brackets, as in this extract:

The students – those without permits – are only allowed to stay twelve months.

In informal writing a dash may replace a full stop.

Turn to Oral practice 2

Oral practice

1 Read out these sentences and say where you could put a dash.

   a) It is Sunday afternoon the whole town half asleep.
   b) We look forward to hearing you've arrived write with all the gory details.
   c) No-one believes what the papers say absolutely no-one at all.
   d) We've had some good weather what a change from last week.
   e) Don't bother to send a cheque it can wait for a month or two.

2 Read out these sentences and say where you could put a dash. In one of them a pair of dashes is needed.

   a) We went to Versailles yesterday so artificial and uninspiring.
   b) This will be a fight take cover quickly!
   c) I really like to fight a quiet life is boring.
   d) I've been struggling with the horses they've become restive.
   e) My friends apart from Diana are very peaceable creatures.

Dash 49

Self-test

These sentences are all taken from letters, and the writing is informal. Where could you use a dash? Write out the words on either side.

a) Enclosed is a note from Martha what an amazing woman she is.
b) I like it here no lions or tigers.
c) I'll be back don't say that I shan't before the children leave.
d) Margaret wants me to return says it will do me good.
e) The hotel is empty guests frightened off by the food!
f) We went to a big wild cattle hacienda a strange and desolate place.

Answers on page 46

Self-test answers

1. a) Nant-y-dugoed is in the county of Montgomery; Stanwardine-in-the-Fields is in neighbouring Shropshire.
   b) The three-man gang was caught red-handed in the local co-op store.
   c) One-word answers are all that is needed in the next round of the quiz.
   d) My brother-in-law is an ex-criminal; he served a nine-year sentence in Parkhurst Prison.
   e) The anti-vivisection lobby clashed with police in Parliament Square.

Prefixes
Hyphens

Quick reference

A *prefix* is added to the front of a word to change or modify the meaning.

EXAMPLES: *sub*marine; *out*classed

Sometimes it is joined to the word by a *hyphen*.

EXAMPLES: *ex*-soldier; *pre*-war

A *hyphen* is also used to join two full words together.

EXAMPLES: a free-standing stove
                old-fashioned medicines

Information

Hyphen comes from a Greek word meaning "together". It is a short line (-) which helps to make meanings or pronunciation clearer. It may do any of the following things:

1 Connect a prefix to the front of a word

A prefix is a syllable placed in front of a word to change the meaning. For example:
a post-war house
re-cycled paper

he is pro-American but anti-Yank (anti = against)
the co-operative movement
an ante-natal clinic (ante = before; natal = birth)

Note that many prefixes are used without a hyphen:

unhappy (you don't see un-happy)
preview
upgrade

2 **Connect two words which have a special meaning when used together**

built-in cupboards   good-looking   the cow-shed
duty-free tobacco   a hip-flask   so-called heroes
a part-time cleaner walking-stick   our living-room

3 **Connect two-word numbers**

twenty-one and ninety-nine

4 **Connect a number to a noun when they are used as an adjective (= describing word**

a tenth-century castle
a second-rate pianist

5 **Help you to make up super-words that you like the sound of**

I dislike his look-at-me-I'm-perfect look.
That was a never-to-be-forgotten birthday party.

THE BASIC RULE: use a hyphen to help readers understand what you have written. When to use them often depends on usage (what people usually do). In many cases they are optional, e.g.

Christlike } both are correct
Christ-like }

Oral practice

1 Which words in these sentences could be joined by a hyphen?

   a) The pre Raphaelite painters were interested in thirteenth century themes; they expressed them in a non realistic way.
   b) A heart shaped table of Anglo French origin was barely visible in the smoke laden atmosphere.

Prefixes, Hyphens

c) All dog lovers should avoid house warming parties organized by cat lovers.
d) He was a self made man who had pursued wealth in a single minded way. His wife accompanied him. She wore a mother of pearl necklace and a primrose coloured costume.

2 Where could you use hyphens in the following passage?

A paper thin partition divided the two rooms in the top flat of the five storey building. As he was highly strung it needed all his powers of self control to prevent him from complaining to the manager about the loud voiced couple arguing in the next room of the jerry built apartment.

3 What about the following sentence? Where might hyphens be placed?

Thirty seven high and mighty sun worshippers were spoon fed with ill assorted ideas about playing pitch and putt in the Olympics.

Self-test

1 Write out the following sentences inserting hyphens and any other punctuation marks where necessary.
   a) Nant y dugoed is in the county of Montgomery Stanwardine in the Fields is in neighbouring Shropshire
   b) the three man gang was caught red handed in the local co op store
   c) one word answers are all that is needed in the next round of the quiz
   d) my brother in law is an ex criminal he served a nine year sentence in parkhurst prison
   e) the anti vivisection lobby clashed with police in parliament square

Answers on page 49

2 Here is a list of prefixes. With the aid of a dictionary find out what they mean and write down beside each one two words that use the particular prefix. Then make up sentences for each word.
   e.g. *Ex* means former. He met his ex-headmaster at the races.
   Check in the dictionary where the prefix is hyphenated to the root word.

   pro- bi- ex- ambi- anti- ante- contra- socio- post- vice- non- dis- electro-

Business letters

Quick reference

A business letter gives information or asks for it. Take care over

spelling
handwriting
punctuation
layout

especially if applying for a job. Employers form their first impression of you from the letter you write. There are particular ways to set out a business letter, with attention to punctuation.

Information

Look at the letter on the following page from a girl who is applying for a job: Notice the five points indicated, and keep them in mind for the future:

(1) Your address, top right
(2) The date beneath it
(3) The name and address of the person you are writing to, above the letter, left
(4) The letter begins a short distance from the margin
(5) Yours faithfully, – capital Y – small f – final comma

Note Not all business letters are set out exactly in this way, but this is probably the simplest "correct" form for you to practise and learn.

Turn to Oral practice 1

54 Business letters

```
                                    (1)  99 Ongar Hill
                                         Blackmore
                                         Essex

                                    (2)  14.7.'80

(3)  The Personnel Manager
     Jones Electrical Co. Ltd.
     Southend SS44


     Dear Sir
(4)       Thank you for your letter dated 12 July.
     Having read the job description carefully I am
     interested in applying for the vacancy. I shall
     be happy to attend for interview on Friday 24 July
     at 4 p.m. as you request.
                              (5)  Yours faithfully,

                                        Arabella Hopeful
```

Turn to Practice 1

If you write a letter about something important, where it may be useful to know exactly what you said, make a copy to keep yourself.

Turn to Practice 2 and 3

Note If you write to someone by name (Dear Mr Booth,) you normally end: *Yours sincerely,* A personal letter to a friend ends almost as you wish. For example: Yours, Yours with love, Cheers, See you soon

Business letters 55

Oral practice

1 Working in pairs, each of you writes a letter to the other applying for a job. Your partner then criticises the letter. You will have to discuss first what kind of job you are applying for – it needn't be too serious but the letter should have all the necessary information and be properly set out.

2 You have bought an item, which is faulty, from a shop. Write a letter to the shopkeeper, explaining when the purchase was made, what was wrong with it and what you want the shop to do about it, e.g. do you want your money back or the item replaced?

3 Work in pairs for this exercise: one of you write the reply from the shopkeeper to the letter in 2, in which he tries to avoid admitting responsibility. Then continue the correspondence, taking it in turns to write the letters. Both writers should remain polite for as long as possible!

Self-test

1 Write a letter to the manager of the local Water Board complaining that the water pressure is low. You should include full details, which may be humorous, about the inconvenience this is causing to your family.

2 Write a short letter to the personnel officer of a local factory asking for a vacation job. Make sure you give all the information she could reasonably ask for.

3 Write out the following addresses as they should appear at the top of a business letter.
   a) 26 Grafton Street Stratford-upon-Avon Warwickshire WR2 3KL
   b) The Cottages Glenfield Nr Tetbury Gloucestershire SW2 5NL
   c) Wednesbury School Stratton Street Birmingham BM3 5TP
   d) Global Products 112–17 Granger Avenue Norwich Norfolk NW7 2ST

56 Business letters

4 Use any of the following as the starting point for a letter of application for a job. Check your letters or headings with the example given in this chapter, noting the five points on page 53.

**BROMPTON HOSPITAL
PIPE FITTER**

Required in the Engineers Department at this specialist hospital. Applicants should hold City & Guilds Certificate in Pipefitting and be experienced and fully conversant in all aspects of plant maintenance, including boilers, pumps, heating plant and air conditioning. Suit young college leaver.

Apply in writing: Personnel Department
Brompton Hospital
Lee Valley Road
SOUTHAMPTON SO2 1DZ

**TRAINEE
TELEX OPERATOR**
(aged 16-18)

with pleasant personality, required for shipping company. Must have pass in GCE "O" level English & accurate typing with min speed of 35 wpm. Good salary to suitably-qualified applicant.

Please write:
Mr K Old
J Drummond Ltd
Halifax Road
HULL

**TRAINEE
CLERK**

For our busy Sub Post Office in Streatham Vale. Full training given. 35 hour week, Wednesday afternoon off with occasional Saturday work. Suit 16-17 year old School Leaver with Maths and English 'O' Level or good CSEs, salary by arrangement.

Please apply: Mrs Goodbody
Central Post Office
Streatham
London SW16

YOUNG PERSON

17 or thereabout required for motor cycle spares department. Good arithmetic and handwriting essential. Five-day week with Saturday working.

Apply: Roy Smith Motors
116-24 Burlington Road
Henley-on-Thames
Oxfordshire

CLERK

For busy Medical Records Dept in a small friendly hospital near Piccadilly. Varied duties for those able to deal tactfully with patients under pressure. Some typing useful. Previous experience an advantage. Salary a.a.e. from £3398-£4793 inc (increase pending). Apply in writing giving full details to Mary Gregory, Records Dept. Royal National Throat Nose and Ear Hospital. Golden Square. Manchester 11.

RECEPTIONIST

High level in English. Good standard of spelling. Will involve telephone work, filing, copy writing, liaising with different offices, normal office duties. This position is urgently required. Please write to:

Miss J. Crichling
The Guardian
99-101, London Road, Morden, Surrey

Self-test answers

1 a) i.e. b) etc. c) e.g. d) etc.

2 a) e.g. b) i.e. c) etc. d) e.g.

Cutting it short

Quick reference

e.g. means "for example":
  I like sweet things, e.g. pudding and biscuits.

i.e. means "that is":
  He pleaded poverty, i.e. lack of cash.

etc. means "and other such things":
  Bring a knife, fork etc. so we can have a picnic.

Information

An abbreviation is a short way of writing something down, in order to save time. Here are three useful ones:

e.g.   The letters e.g. mean *for example*, as in these two sentences:

  The radio telescope tracked the course of the early space satellites, e.g. Sputnik I, Lunik I and Explorer I.

  The guide showed them many of the sights of London, e.g. St Paul's Cathedral, the Tower and the House of Commons.

You may wonder why the letters *e.g.* mean *for example*. They are the initials of *exempli gratia*, which means *for example* in Latin.

Turn to Oral practice 1 and 2

i.e.   This abbreviation means *that is*, as in the following examples:

  She brought all the tools she needed, i.e. a plane, a saw, a set of chisels and a small vice.

Abbreviations

> The foreign secretary visited four South American countries last year, i.e. Venezuela, Peru, Bolivia and Chile.

The initials stand for the Latin words, *id est* (= it is).

Turn to Oral practice 3 and 4

etc. This is perhaps the commonest abbreviation of all. The precise meaning varies, depending on the context. Usually it means *and others too*. Here are examples:

> The encyclopaedia gives important facts about the lives of notable people; where they were born; what kind of training they received, etc.

> He sells books, newspapers, magazines, etc.

Again, the origin is Latin. *Etc.* are the first three letters of *et cetera*, meaning *and the others*.

Turn to Oral practice 5 and 6

Oral practice

1 Read out these sentences, putting in e.g. in the appropriate place. It is perfectly correct to read it out as *"for example"*.
   a) The caretaker dislikes awkward tenants, those who bang doors late at night.
   b) He makes money in unusual ways by collecting bottle tops and selling them to sculptors in metal.
   c) The king gave land to loyal tenants those who had supported him in battle.
   d) She has experienced some unusual holidays camel trekking in the Sahara desert.

2 Make up three sentences, in each of which the abbreviation e.g. is used. You can, if you wish, begin the first one like this:

   He hides his money in unexpected places . . . .

3 Two of these sentences can be written to include the abbreviation *i.e.* Which ones and where should the *i.e.* be placed?

a) We made a pact to write to each other every week.
b) He said it was homogeneous made of a single substance.
c) The original humbugs were unusual in taste very sweet but never sickly.
d) Nobody likes cakes which have been in the shop for a couple of weeks.

4 Make up three sentences of your own, using i.e.

5 Shorten each of these sentences by the use of the abbreviation 'etc'.

   a) He brought home the electric fire, light bulbs, switches, batteries, torches, bedside lamps, lampshades and plugs.
   b) The drawing room was furnished with comfortable chairs, thick carpets, mahogany furniture, tapestries, a solid copper fire guard and two leather settees.
   c) The jeweller's window displayed brooches, rings, necklaces, bracelets, earrings and watches.

6 Read out these sentences, putting the appropriate abbreviation in the place of the dash.

   a) Bring the kitchen utensils: pots, pans –.
   b) I dislike places where animals are confined for people's pleasure, – zoological gardens.
   c) The old railway engines, – those driven by steam, were often as fast as the average diesel engine today.

Self-test

1 Which abbreviation is needed for each of the gaps in these sentences?

   a) The inhabitants of this particular mountainous country ... Switzerland, are extremely patriotic.
   b) You need a snowstorm of documents to visit Indonesia: passport, vaccination certificate, visas . . . .
   c) Do not mark these examination papers in inappropriate places . . . a tube train in the rush hour.
   d) The Quechua people of Peru are fond of ceremonies: weddings, temple feasts, cremations . . . .

2 Which abbreviations are needed for the gaps in these sentences?

60 Abbreviations

a) The mountain rescue team expects to bring a hundred useful things, ... blankets and vacuum flasks.
b) He met the leader ... the woman who decided the main lines of approach.
c) Make the arrangements: booking tickets, reserve seats ....
d) You can buy many different kinds of recordings of Asian music, ... the music of a Balinese gamelan.

Answers on page 56

Self-test answers

1 I picked up my two heavy suitcases and with a grimace I walked on, feeling as though the last hundred yards would stretch my arms permanently beyond their normal length. I did not have to run any more. That was some consolation. I heard a cry and looked round. It was my Polish acquaintance. He started to shout at me.

2 The new road will run just behind the garden. No doubt it will take several months to complete and will cause a great deal of mess. The mess is bearable. The noise, on the other hand, cannot be ignored. Perhaps one gets used to it. After all, some people live by a busy railway. In any case it will be worth it in the end.

3 The town is on a spit of land between the harbour and a beach. The roads are incredibly narrow and chock-a-block with holiday-makers. You can drive your car through during the summer, but only at five in the morning. Cornish pasties are sold. Some are a disgrace, containing potato and swede and nothing much else. Complaints are greeted with blank stares. One can buy good pasties but they must be searched for. I would like to go there again, but in winter.

Revision

How much have you learned from this *Checkbook*? Here is a selection of passages from various sources on which you can test your knowledge of all the punctuation points covered in this book. Rewrite each passage putting in the appropriate punctuation. When you have finished, compare your versions with those of others in your group. There is not necessarily a right or wrong answer, but if you can't agree on a point, look it up in the relevant section and *talk* about any differences you come across.

Remember to copy out words carefully and write clearly as you work through these passages. You will sometimes need to put in *paragraphs* to make better sense of the extracts, and keep in mind the different *styles* of writing to be found in an advertisement or a short story or a recipe which affect how you might punctuate it.

1 Recipe

first melt the butter in a large heavy pan then add the onion and cook gently until golden about 10 minutes taking care that they dont burn or catch on the bottom add the sherry vegetables fruit spices and seasoning to the pan place a double thickness of greaseproof paper which has been well dampened with cold water first over the ingredients and cover the pan with a lid simmer very gently for 1 hour checking from time to time that nothing is sticking after that add the stock to the contents of the pan first removing the paper and stir everything now transfer the soup in two batches to a liquidiser and blend then press the soup through a sieve to remove pips and stalks and return to a clean pan re-heat check the seasoning ladle into warmed soup bowls and garnish each serving with an apple slice and some snipped chives

2 Ghost story

not so long ago a haunted house stood near dokkum every night on the stroke of twelve there was a most terrible noise in one of its bedrooms no-one would sleep in that room and all the furniture had been removed from it except an old bed the people who lived in the house had tried to find out what caused this unearthly noise but since no-one was brave enough to stay in the room at night it remained a mystery one evening, when it had been raining for a week a little old woman came to the door the trees were dripping the streets were flooded water ran in a swift stream down the road the leaden skies seemed to have endless rain left in them the fields had begun to look like lakes and it was difficult to get about the poor woman was soaked to the skin rain dripped from her hair on to her shoulders her shoes squished with water she had tried to put her skirt over her head as a kind of umbrella but that was soaked, too she was timid about knocking on the door but she thought the people who live here can only tell me to go away thats the worst they can do

3 Magazine interview

sylvester stallone ducked and weaved like a professional prize fighter his handsome head jiggling from side to side the midnight black hair lifting and settling like a slow motion commercial big fists bunched the threshold of pain he said thats what fascinates me until youve actually been hit by a full blown heavyweight contender you dont understand this kind of inflicted pain stallone understands he has certainly suffered for his art more than 150 stitches in one film in the end i was getting such severe headaches and memory loss that doctors tried to warn me off doing it again but this last time wasnt so bad well i broke my nose twice my own brother hit me and no one spars harder than your own brother but thats the name of the game right

4 Television previews

WIMBLEDON '82

bbc2 130 get the lunch over early today to watch one of the sporting highlights of the year the mens singles final between the grunter jimmy connors and the groaner john mcenroe weather permitting it should be a great occasion it is still the worlds most prestigious tennis crown and whatever antics take place on court that most gentlemanly of commentators dan maskell will try to calm us with his controlled enthusiasm even at moments of high excitement dan never raises his voice but he has been known to chuckle with admiration and he can get more emotion into a simple phrase like i say what an absolutely marvellous return than any other commentator i know

CARAVAN TO VACCARES

itv 930 this slick adventure yarn colourfully set in the camargue region of france is about a footloose american david birney hired to smuggle an east european scientist into the us on the way he picks up a british photographer charlotte rampling and runs into trouble with a gang who want to kidnap the scientist

THE DAME OF SARK
itv 815 even more stiff british upperlip as celia johnson in the title role copes with the occupation of the island tony britton is the nice german commandant and simon cadell now better known as the wet entertainments officer of hi de hi is the nasty nazi

5 Lucky stars

CANCER
june 22 july 22 at work your actions are being noticed and you will gain or lose accordingly if you spend the weekend in company life will be hectic you need some time to yourself be certain you get it

PISCES
feb 19 march 20 you can ask a favour and probably get a positive response officials may be prepared to bend rules if you are trying to cheat someone however youll land in trouble romance with a steady partner should improve if you both show willing

LIBRA
sept 23 oct 23 a chance to improve your work prospects but it must be balanced against responsibilities at home this could be a flirtatious week there could be the chance of something free plus an invitation to somewhere unusual lucky day wednesday

SCORPIO
oct 24 nov 22 dont neglect a relative who has been poorly or out of luck even if you arent the best of friends perhaps you are being too cautious in a money matter dont expect miracles if youre waiting for a debt to be repaid

VIRGO
aug 24 sept 22 avoid wasting funds on trivial items you should plan your finances more sensibly especially for long term saving there could be a separation that proves helpful indeed it could bring you closer to someone else try to get away at the weekend

6 Newspaper article

day out in a bunker
a county council is offering families guided tours of a nuclear bunker to demonstrate its failings the bunker which would become an emergency planning sub headquarters in the event of a nuclear war is under cusworth

hall museum near doncaster and contains equipment which in some cases dates back to the first world war mr norman west the chairman of south yorkshires anti nuclear working party said there are telephone exchanges down there which would be better sited in the museum above the teleprinters are so old that i understand there are now two people left in the country with the necessary expertise to repair them mr west added that the labour controlled council wanted to lift the secrecy surrounding britains nuclear war preparations the bunker will be opened on july 5 councillors and council officials will be on hand to guide visitors around

7 Help the Aged advertisement

Keep an old woman on the streets
because she is elderly ella 78 has a choice of whom she talks to mostly its the budgie sometimes the cat of course if shes really desperate she can always buy some conversation by taking a bus into town and talking to the driver its this kind of grinding loneliness which can wear down the spirit of old people quicker than all their aches and pains help the aged are actively making sure that as many old people as possible get out of their homes and into day centres where they can meet new friends and become involved in new hobbies and projects your help is needed £80 would buy a road fund licence for a minibus £1000 a wheelchair lift £11000 a new specially equipped mini bus but even £5 towards the upkeep of a day centre would be a welcome contribution

8 Book extract

the weather cleared as we drove into weston and we halted on the promenade the seaside they said we gazed around us but saw no sign of the sea we saw a vast blue sky and an infinity of mud stretching away to the shadows of wales but rousing smells of an invisible ocean astonished our land locked nostrils salt and wet weeds and fishy oozes a sharp difference in every breath our deep ditched valley had not prepared us for this for we had never seen such openness the blue windy world seemed to have blown quite flat bringing the sky to the level of our eyebrows canvas booths flapped on the edge of the prom mouths crammed with shellfish and vinegar there were rows of prim boarding houses each the size of our vicarage bath chairs carriages and donkeys and stilted far out on the rippled mud a white pier like a sleeping dragon

from *Cider with Rosie* by Laurie Lee
(Chatto and Windus)